Awesome Asian Animals

A+ books

Giant Pandas Are

by Megan Cooley Peterson

Consultant: Jackie Gai, DVM
Wildlife Vet

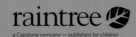

raintree
a Capstone company — publishers for children

Raintree is an imprint of Capstone Global Library Limited, a company incorporated in England and Wales having its registered office at 7 Pilgrim Street, London, EC4V 6LB – Registered company number: 6695582

www.raintree.co.uk
myorders@raintree.co.uk

Edited by Michelle Hasselius
Designed by Peggie Carley
Picture research by Tracy Cummins
Production by Morgan Walters
Printed and bound in China.

ISBN 978-1-474-70251-5
19 18 17 16 15
10 9 8 7 6 5 4 3 2 1

British Library Cataloguing in Publication Data
A full catalogue record for this book is available from the British Library.

Acknowledgements
Capstone Press: 16; Getty Images: Glowimages, 18 Bottom, Joe Petersburger, 14 Top, Keren Su, 18 Top; iStockphoto: mchen007, 21 Top, 22 L, mrbfaust, 14 Bottom, Rchang, 11, samkee, 4, yesfoto, 10; Minden Pictures: Cyril Ruoso, 20, 21 Bottom, Katherine Feng, 13 Bottom, 24, 25, Konrad Wothe, 17, Thomas Marent, 12 Bottom, Tony Heald/npl, 28; Shutterstock: Eric Isselee, Cover L, Cover Top R, Cover Back, 1, 26 Left, 30, 32, Hung Chung Chih, Cover Bottom, 6, 8, 19, 22 R, 26 R, 29 Top, leungchopan, 9, lzf, 29 Bottom, nattanan726, 12 Top, 15, Rigamondis, Design Element, Sergey Dzyuba, 7, silverjohn, 23, 27, TonyV3112, 5.

We would like to thank Jackie Gai, DVM, for her invaluable help in the preparation of this book.

Every effort has been made to contact copyright holders of material reproduced in this book. Any omissions will be rectified in subsequent printings if notice is given to the publisher.

All the internet addresses (URLs) given in this book were valid at the time of going to press. However, due to the dynamic nature of the internet, some addresses may have changed, or sites may have changed or ceased to exist since publication. While the author and publisher regret any inconvenience this may cause readers, no responsibility for any such changes can be accepted by either the author or the publisher.

Contents

Bonkers for bamboo 4

A giant panda's body. 8

Life in the mountains. 16

Growing up 24

Saving giant pandas. 28

Glossary 30
Books 31
Websites 31
Comprehension questions 31
Index. 32

Bonkers for bamboo

A giant panda yanks down a bamboo stem. The panda sits on its hind legs and holds the bamboo with its front paws. The panda plucks leaves from the bamboo. Then it grinds the leaves and stem with its teeth.

Giant pandas spend about 14 hours a day eating bamboo. Adult pandas eat 9 to 18 kilograms (20 to 40 pounds) of bamboo a day. These mammals' stomachs can't break down plants very well. To get enough nutrients, pandas need to eat a lot of bamboo.

A giant panda's body

What's black and white and furry all over? A giant panda! Giant pandas have white heads with black eye patches and black ears. They also have black arms and legs. White fur covers a short tail.

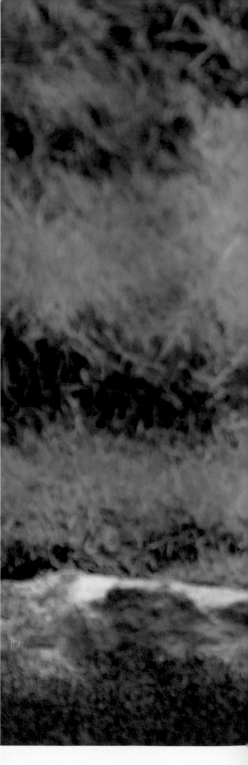

Giant pandas belong to the bear family. Adults weigh up to 113 kilograms (250 pounds). They are up to 0.9 metres (3 feet) tall at the shoulders.

Giant pandas have small, dark eyes that see well. Unlike most bears, pandas do not have round pupils. They have narrow, cat-like pupils. In China the giant panda is called a bear cat.

A giant panda uses its sense of smell to help it in the wild. Pandas use their noses to find food and other pandas. Young pandas use their noses to sniff out dangerous animals, such as the golden cat and yellow-throated marten. But adult pandas have few predators.

Giant pandas have five strong claws on each paw. They also have a long wrist bone in each front paw. These bones help pandas to grasp bamboo.

Open wide! A giant panda has strong jaws and 42 teeth for eating bamboo. Sharp front teeth slice the tough plant. The panda's back teeth crush and chew.

Life in the mountains

All wild giant pandas live in the bamboo forests of central China. Pandas prefer cool, wet forests high in the mountains.

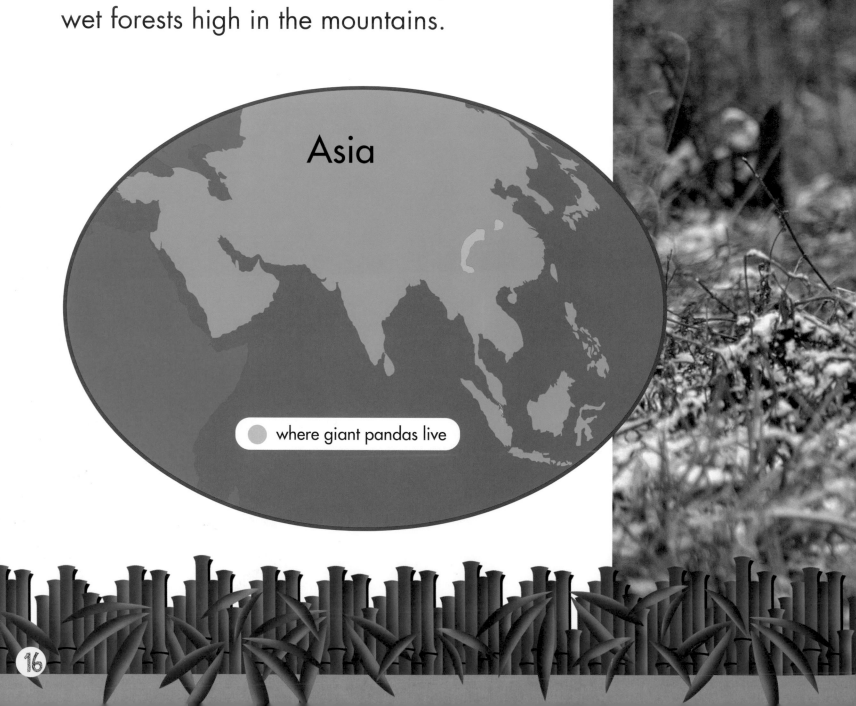

Asia

where giant pandas live

Giant pandas do not hibernate like other bears. In colder months they move to lower areas of the mountains, where it's warmer.

Giant pandas live alone, except when mothers are raising cubs. Adults have their own home ranges. A panda uses its scent to communicate with other giant pandas. Pandas rub their bodies against trees. They scrape trees and the ground with their claws. Their scents let other pandas know where they've been.

Giant pandas don't roar like other bears. But they do make lots of sounds. Pandas huff and snort when upset. They bleat like lambs to say hello. Females bark at males when it's time to mate.

Giant pandas communicate with their bodies. They lower their heads and stare at other pandas to scare them away. Pandas cover their eye patches with their paws when they're afraid. When it's time to play, pandas roll around on the ground.

Giant pandas spend most of their days looking for and eating bamboo. Bamboo gives pandas most of the water they need. But they also drink water from rivers and streams. To save energy, pandas don't travel very far each day.

Giant pandas curl up under trees to sleep.
Sometimes they snooze high up in the trees.
Pandas sleep from two to six hours at a time.

Growing up

Female giant pandas give birth to one or two cubs in autumn. Cubs weigh about 142 grams (5 ounces) at birth. They are 18 centimetres (7 inches) long. That's about as long as a tube of toothpaste!

Newborn panda cubs can't see or hear. They have pink skin and not much fur. Cubs stay warm by snuggling up to their mothers. By the winter, cubs have grown a full coat of fur.

Giant panda cubs love to play. They climb on their mothers and swat at them. Mothers nuzzle their cubs. They also teach their cubs how to find and eat bamboo. Cubs stay with their mothers for about three years. Giant pandas live for about 20 years in the wild.

Saving giant pandas

When bamboo forests are cut down, pandas don't have enough food to eat. Roads and towns make it hard for pandas to move to new forests. Because of this, giant pandas are endangered. Fewer than 2,500 pandas live in the wild.

Today, zoos breed giant pandas. In the wild, land is set aside for pandas to live on. People want to save these awesome Asian animals.

Glossary

breed mate and produce young

cub young animal such as a panda, cheetah, lion or tiger

endangered in danger of dying out

hibernate spend winter in a deep sleep

mammal warm–blooded animal that breathes air; mammals have hair or fur

mate join together to produce young

nutrient substance living things need to stay healthy

predator animal that hunts another animal for food

pupil dark centre of the eye that lets in light

range area where an animal mainly lives

Books

Animal Infographics, Chris Oxlade (Raintree, 2014)

Animals in Danger in Asia, Richard and Louise Spilsbury (Raintree, 2013)

China: A Benjamin Blog and His Inquistive Dog Guide (Country Guides), Anita Ganeri (Raintree, 2014)

Websites

www.bbc.co.uk/nature/life/Giant_Panda
Learn interesting facts about giant pandas.

http://gowild.wwf.org.uk/asia
Find out fun facts about Asian animals, read stories and make your own panda mask!

www.ngkids.co.uk/did-you-know/ten-panda-facts
What do pandas like to eat for dinner? Find this answer and more!

Comprehension questions

1. Giant pandas have their own ranges. What is a range?

2. Giant pandas use their bodies to communicate with other pandas. How does a panda tell others it is scared?

3. Giant pandas are endangered. What are people doing to try to save the giant panda?

Index

arms 8

bamboo 4, 6, 12, 14, 16, 22, 26, 28

bears 9, 10, 17, 20

China 10, 16

claws 12, 18

colours 8, 25

communication 18, 20, 21
  body 21
  scents 18
  sounds 20

cubs 18, 24, 25, 26

eyes 8, 10, 21

habitat 16, 28

head 8, 21

legs 4, 8

life span 26

paws 4, 12, 21

predators 11

sense of smell 11

size 9, 24

tail 8

teeth 4, 14

zoos 29